Dreams

The Supernatural Portal into the Past, Present, and Future

Dreams

The Supernatural Portal into the Past, Present, and Future

Carlos Turner

J. Kenkade
PUBLISHING®
LITTLE ROCK, ARKANSAS

J. Kenkade Publishing
6104 Forbing Rd
Little Rock, AR 72209
www.jkenkadepublishing.com
Facebook.com/jkenkadepublishing

J. Kenkade Publishing is a registered trademark.

Printed in the United States of America
ISBN 978-1-944486-78-5

Table of Contents

Dedication

I'm dedicating this book to My Mother,
Marie Turner-Coleman!
Thank you Moma for pushing me to be
the best in all that I do.

INTRODUCTION

As we evolve as eternal Spirits learning how to function in this world as humans, we are always going to be forever learning and researching things about the supernatural. There's one supernatural experience that happens almost to everyone in the earth realm and this experience is call dreaming!

Albert Einstein said that his theory of relativity originated from a dream he experienced from a young age. George Patton, who was a military general, said he received military guidance from his dreams. Pastor A.J. Gordon once said, "We are most awake to the things of the spirit when we are sleep to the world!"

It has always been on the heart of the father to help us to make contact with his World (spirit realm), and he in turn makes contact with our world (physical realm).So Jesus makes a powerful statement in his teaching concerning prayer. In Matthew 6:10 he said pray…."Thy Kingdom come, thy will be done in earth, as it is in heaven." In other words, give us access to your world in the world we live in! What a Powerful prayer to pray!

I believe it's very imperative that the people of God all over the world would crave and desire to tap into this realm from which we all came! All things started in the spirit, and all things will end in the spirit, so it's important to know something about the spirit realm and its operations!

What we need to understand is, dreams can expose you to realms, dimensions, and spheres of the spirit and the entire universe! Because this is a spiritual tool it's not limited to time zones, so he will reveal things in the:

Past - (Gen. 20:1-18)
Present – (Acts 9:10-16) (Gen. 28:12)
Future - (Matt. 1:18-23)

The Prophet Hosea said in his writings in chapter 4:6, "My people are destroyed for a lack of knowledge! Let's not limited ourselves to the natural realm and learn how to make contact with the spirit realm! You don't have to wait to die or transition to make contact with this realm, dreams are one of the portals to the realm of the spirit.

Chapter 1

✝

THE QUESTION IS:
WHAT IS A DREAM?

Dream– It is a combination of images, thoughts, and emotions working together to create a movie-like event with known & unknown persons, places, and things that reveal direction, instructions, and warnings in the earth realm while you are asleep.

The father has given us this heavenly instrument of Dreams to deliver saints from drastic situations that could have cost them their lives! The father has designed this spiritual system so that every spirit can have access to information concerning their past, present, and future information through Dreams. (Thank you, Lord!!)

Hosea 4:6– People are destroyed for a lack of knowledge.

James 1:5– If a man lacks Wisdom (information, direction, and instruction) let him ask God!

So, if I lack knowledge of information about something, the wise thing to do is to ask GOD! There's nothing wrong with asking God questions, especially when you need to know what to do! Sometimes he will answer you through dreams!

Dreaming is connected to the prophetic, and sometimes the father will show you in a dream (Visual) instead of speaking to you audibly. Both dreaming and Prophecy have the capacity to do the same thing, so many biblical scholars believe that dreaming is a form of first level Prophecy!

Prophetic– Reveals and Confirms
Dreams– Reveal and Confirm

Some saints claim that God no longer speaks through the supernatural vehicle of dreams. They believe that God only spoke to the Apostles in supernatural dreams, Visions, and by angelic appearances. This religious way of thinking is NOT biblical! The bible teaches that God gave dreams and Visions to both Saints and sinners alike!

(Acts 9:10-16, Judg. 7:13-15, Dan. 5:1-31, Gen. 41:1-8)

Notes

_____

_____

_____

_____

_____

_____

_____

_____

_____

_____

_____

_____

_____

_____

_____

_____

Chapter 2

✝

SLEEP AND WARFARE

God has so much wisdom to impart to us, both for our personal lives and for the work he has appointed us to do. Some of that wisdom comes when we are asleep because our eyes can't see, nor our minds comprehend what God is trying to say to us sometimes! As I stated once before, the spirit man is most alert when you are asleep! Therefore, if we fail to heed our dreams, we miss so many instructions and directions the father is trying to convey to us!

We must erase the attitude that dreams are insignificant and not worth our attention.

Don't be deceived! Answers come through dreams, but we must get some rest and go to sleep. Why? Because you can't dream if you don't sleep.

Sleep was designed by God as a Ministry tool to:

1. Rest your physical body
2. Daily awaken you to the things of the spirit via dreams
3. To see what we need to know or do

Sleep – was designed by the father, not just to rest your physical body, but to be used also as an instrument of Power to transfer his agenda (his will) into your spirit through dreams while you're asleep *It must be embraced as a weapon*

2 Cor. 10:4 – "For the weapons of our warfare are not carnal but mighty through God..."

Let's look at Job 33:14-16. "For God speaks once, yea twice, yet man perceive it not. In a dream, in a vision of the night, when "DEEP SLEEP" falleth upon men, in slumbering upon the bed; Then he openeth their ears of men, and sealeth their instructions!

So, it's safe to say that the purpose for our dreams is to make up for something God was trying to convey, but we couldn't hear it or comprehend it!

What we must understand is the devil understands that in order to get instruction or a warning from the father when our ear is still in training, he has to keep us from experiencing deep sleep!

I believe supernatural things happen when you are able to experience "Deep Sleep."

Adam's answer was always in him, but after he experienced deep sleep, it was revealed (Eve)! (Gen. 2:20)

Deep Sleep– Hebrew (Tar'de'mah)

Spiritual Warfare is engaged to keep you from Deep Sleep

The fight is against DEEP SLEEP!

The enemy uses these 3 things to keep you up at night so you won't experience deep sleep, and so he can keep you away from what you need for your life:

1. Worry– Allowing situations to stay on your mind that you can't control

2. Wrestling– Struggling with old appetites and ways of doing of things

3. Work– Staying busy, but not productive

These are weapons of mass destruction when it comes to getting you some rest and getting some good sleep! But Decree this with me today, NO WEAPON!! (Isa. 54:17)

Notes

_____

_____

_____

_____

_____

_____

_____

_____

_____

_____

_____

_____

_____

_____

_____

_____

_____

_____

_____

_____

_____

_____

_____

_____

_____

_____

_____

_____

_____

_____

_____

_____

_____

_____

_____

_____

_____

_____

_____

_____

_____

_____

_____

_____

_____

Chapter 3

✝

MIND YOUR BUSINESS

It's very important to understand that portals of all kinds are constantly opening and closing throughout your day. Not knowing how to close and lock portals can affect your dream state. (Deut. 30:19)

SET– Naw'than– (appointed, put into motion)

4 Portals:

Life– Hebrew "Chay"– a "Community" = A connection of many parts to make one whole, healthy, and prosperous.

Death– Hebrew "Ma'veth"– Separated and

at a place of ruins.

Cursing– Hebrew "Kel-aw-law'- Abuse (Physical, Mental, Spiritual, Emotional, etc.)

Blessing– Hebrew "Ber-aw-kaw"- A Treaty of Peace!

What is a Treaty?- an official agreement made between 2 or more Countries or Kingdoms! (Heaven and Earth)

So, what does this have to do with dreams you may be asking? You must be careful of the portals you entertain! Watch this…

How does a dream occur?

Ecclesiastes 5:3 "For a dream cometh through the multitude of business;"

Business- Hebrew (In'yawn) – "occupied by" "employment"

In other words, what you have *entertained, allowed, hired, or employed* to come into your spirit.

Whatever you allow to make penetration into your spirit will determine whether you will have a (Godly) dream or an (ungodly) dream. This is important because not all dreams come from God! So it's important we understand Eph. 4:27– that says "Give no place (Greek- Topos- a License) to the devil!"

To close demonic Portals that affect your mind and thoughts, especially when you are asleep, it's important you use your mouth!

2 Cor. 10:5 "Casting down imaginations, and every high thing that exalteth itself against the knowledge of God, and bringing into captivity every thought to the obedience of Christ!"

Filter your spirit with prayer every night because you don't need anything to stop you from receiving from God!

Notes

_____

_____

_____

_____

_____

_____

_____

_____

_____

_____

_____

_____

_____

Chapter 4

†

THIS IS ONLY A TEST

Although we now understand that dreams carry power, revelation, information, and warning, we must be wise in pursuit because all Dreams don't come from God, and it's important we know the difference! We must be aware of the danger of accepting without question a dream we had, or some other person claims God has revealed to them for us.

It's very dangerous accepting untested "revelation" especially in the time we currently live in, we must be aware of this.

So, the question is: What are some ways to test the source of our dreams? I don't have all the answers, but here are a few ways:

Ask yourself...

a.) Is it in Agreement with Scripture?– Acts 17:10-11

b.) What's my Inner Witness saying concerning it?– Rom. 8:16, Col. 3:15, Phil. 4:7

c.) Is it bringing Fulfillment?– Deut. 18:21-22, Deut. 13:1-4

That's just a few, but it would also help if one understood the 3 types of dreams before trying to test it to see if it's from God or not!

3 Types of Dreams:

1. *False Dream*– When a Prophet/anybody shares a dream with you in order to get you to either error or to fulfill a desire, plan, and/or idea from the enemy to establish a certain bondage. (Jer. 23:32)

2. *Lying Dream*– A demonic dream you have that suggests potential ideas to you that are totally contrary to the Word of God and his will. (Zech. 10:2-3)

3. *Divine Dream*– A dream given by God in order to order your steps in regard to a certain situation. (Psa. 37:23, Matt. 2:12-13)

So, as you can see, we must carefully test every dream, not in the spirit of fear but in the spirit of accuracy in the things of God! As we all know, we can't afford to waste any more time playing with our lives and future!

Notes

_____

_____

_____

_____

_____

_____

_____

_____

_____

_____

_____

_____

_____

_____

_____

_____

_____

_____

_____

_____

_____

_____

_____

_____

_____

_____

_____

_____

_____

_____

_____

_____

_____

_____

_____

_____

_____

_____

_____

_____

_____

_____

_____

_____

Chapter 5

†

PLEASE CLOSE THE DOOR

We can't talk about dreams if we don't deal with the experience of nightmares! The nightmare is the dark side of the dreaming experience. Feelings of dread, helplessness, and sometimes paralysis in the face of danger accompany nightmares. Nightmares can be very demonic and terrifying. Many actually wake up screaming, which leads many to believe that all senses and emotions are at an all-time high when you are asleep!

Some dream specialists believe that nightmares occur:

1. When a person sleeps on a full stomach

2. When there is a restriction in circulation

3. When there is an irritation of the central nervous system

4. While on certain medications, and the list goes on and on and on.

The question is: What is exactly a nightmare, and how does it occur?

Nightmares– are actually triggered by a person who has lost control of his/her Spirit, Words, Actions, Imagination, and Soul (Will, Mind, and Emotions) and is unaware of the demonic open portals that are operating and fueling their dream state.

Let's look at what the word says in Proverbs 25:28, "He that hath no rule over his own spirit is like a city is broken down, and without walls!"

Rule– Hebrew (Ma'sar)= (control, management) over his/her spirit

The writer uses this illustration because in biblical times they had walls around the whole city so that nothing could get in that city undetected by the watchmen that were on the walls. But he shares that if a man or woman doesn't have control over their spirit, anything can get in. Wow! That's serious as it relates to dreams because many will go to sleep with all kinds of stuff in them, and that's why prayer before sleep is so vital! Why? Because with an OPEN spirit anything can get in! If one doesn't have management over their own spirit, they will find themselves entertaining the demonic spirits that engineered the dream!

Speaking negativity, complaining, and talking too much tore down the walls of Job's spirit and opened up Portals he didn't expect to be open! (Job 7:11, 14-15)

Believe it or not there is another level in the nightmare realm that the body of Christ needs to be aware of, and that's dealing with Incubus & Succubus in Dreams.

*Incubus– A male demon believed to have sexual intercourse with sleeping women.

*Succubus– A female demon believed to have sexual intercourse with sleeping men.

Researchers said these dreaming experiences have caused health problems, mental health issues, and even death for those that continue to have these experiences.

These spirits in the dream-states have left physical bruises, slashes, cuts, and damaged private parts, even to the extent of women not being able to carry a child!

These demons go after Humans (especially women with high sex drives
(The goal is to get humans to Pro-create with them again, as it were in Noah's days.)
(Why?) Luke 17:26, Gen 6:1-4, 2 Cor 11:14, Gen 19:1-4

It's very important that we learn how to rebuild the walls of our spirit, especially if you are experiencing any of these demonic experiences in the nightmare realm!
Jude 1:20, Eph. 6:14-17
Another thing to consider is to filter your spirit so you can start rebuilding!
Psa. 63:6, Psa. 42:8
Not all, but in most cases, if these experiences keep reoccurring, I suggest Deliverance from the attachment of these demonic spirits! Here are 6 reasons why these spirits are attracted to you.
1. *Inheritance*– Forefathers sins, continuing in the sins of our forefathers. This is where we get the term Generational Curses. (Exod.

20:5)

2. *Involvement with unclean and unholy things*– Cursed objects, people, pictures, artifacts, crafts, and paintings. (2 Cor. 6:17, Num. 16:26)

3. *Territorial Rights violations*– Living in a cursed house, living on cursed land or property. (Lev. 14:33-38)

4. *Being attached to stuff used in demonic rituals*– Transfer of a gift, dances people do, occult drawings and tattoos. (Deut. 7:26, Lev. 19:27-28)

5. *Direct Disobedience*- Vows you made to God if he would help or bless you, or he sent a word through a Prophet or his word and you just don't do it. (Mal 3:10)

6. *Sexual Intercourse*- Transmitting and exchanging bloodline curses that haven't been dealt with. (Ezra 10:10-12)

It's not God's will to be tormented by the very thing he created to give us direction in the earth! It's time to get FREE in JESUS NAME!!!!

Notes

_____
_____
_____
_____
_____
_____
_____
_____
_____
_____
_____
_____
_____
_____
_____
_____
_____
_____
_____
_____
_____
_____
_____
_____
_____
_____

Chapter 6

✝

TELL ME WHAT THIS MEANS

The most common problem with understanding dreams is that people don't recognize that dreams speak Symbolic language!! Most people get discouraged about their dreams because they have NO idea what they mean. So, like most they just sweep it under the rug and pay it no attention, not knowing that it could be the very answer to their prayer and/or question! I must admit interpretation can be difficult at times, but I suggest that we spend time with God in Prayer, and he will not steer us wrong!

Let's keep in mind that the Bible is filled with much symbolism, and we must take into consideration so do our dreams. So it's safe to say Symbolism can't be taken literally!

I guess the bottom line is we need to know what the Symbolism represents and what it means. (Rev. 12:1-4, Matt. 16: 6-12)

For instance, dreaming about a snake is not always evil. In the Word of God the snake is a symbol of both GOOD and EVIL!

*Num. 21:8 – a symbol of healing (Good)
*Matt. 10:16 – a symbol of wisdom (Good)
*Gen. 3:1 – a symbol of deception (Evil)

Now let's be clear about dreams, *not all are symbolic.* Some are *literal.*

When we dream of people, we must ask ourselves, "What does this person represent to me?" This is called a Subjective dream (the person may reflect something about ourselves). Sometimes the dream can be an Objective dream, which means it is Literal. This is very rare when it's something coming from God, but very much possible!

Most dreams that came to the Prophets were mostly Subjective and maybe 3% Objective, but those that were Objective, the father came himself in the dream or sent an Angel!

When experiencing Spiritual things, it's very important to understand basic spiritual symbolism in the area of Dreams and even visions.

Here is some basic Symbolism as it relates to Dreams!

Colors:

Red– Color of Transformation, Protection

Orange– Connection getting ready to happen

Yellow– Empty, Vacant = Overwhelmed

Green– Development, Maturity, Growth

Blue– Favor, Spirit, Open portals, Hope

Indigo- Royal, Wealth, Money

Numbers:

0 – Something is going to happen that will complete your life

1 – Beginning/You

2 – Indecision, Witness

3 – Covenant

4 – Stability, Strength, Earth

5 – Grace, Life, Unity

6 – Man, No harmony or balance

7 – Completed, Perfected

8 – New beginning

9 – Birth, Impartation

10 – Rearrangement, Restoration

Shapes:

Square – What is Just and Accurate

Circle – Forever, Without end, Divine

Triangle – What is powerful, Strength, Wisdom

Notes

_____

_____

_____

_____

_____

_____

_____

_____

_____

_____

_____

_____

_____

_____

_____

_____

_____

Chapter 7

✝

WRITE AND WAIT ON IT

The most commonly known problem with dreaming is we don't remember them. This can be a problem when you are trying to get an answer from the father! The most common cause of not remembering your dreams is most people don't give serious attention to them. That's right! When attention is drawn to the fact that dreams are important, a person will usually begin to remember their dreams.

I want to give you a few suggestions that may help you to sharpen your dreaming gift or how to better remember your dreams:

1. Mediate 30 minutes before you go to sleep:

Psa. 63:6 When I remember thee upon my bed, and meditate on thee in the night watches.

2. Take Vitamin E and C, drink 6 glasses of H2O, sleep at least 7hrs:

Dan. 1:12 Prove thy servants, I beseech thee, ten days; and let them give us pulse to eat, and water to drink.

Dan. 1:13 Then let our countenances be looked upon before thee, and the countenance of the children that eat of the portion of the king's meat: and as thou seest, deal with thy servants.

Dan. 1:14 So he consented to them in this matter, and proved them ten days.

Dan. 1:16 Thus Melzar took away the portion of their meat, and the wine that they should drink; and gave them pulse.

Dan. 1:17 As for these four children, God gave them knowledge and skill in all learning and wisdom: and Daniel had understanding in all visions and dreams.

3. Write it Down:

Dan. 7:1 In the first year of Belshazzar king of Babylon Daniel had a dream and visions of his head upon his bed: then he wrote the dream, and told the sum of the matters.

All of these points are very important, but writing down your dreams is very, very Important, especially when you have some things placed on the altar before the Lord.

Even Daniel understood that writing down your dream was a powerful tool even if he had no problem trying to recall them. I suggest as kingdom people that we do the same as we continue to discover the will of God for our lives.

Notes

_____

_____

_____

_____

_____

_____

_____

_____

_____

_____

_____

_____

_____

_____

_____

Chapter 8

†

DREAM GEMS

Here is a list of some Dream Spiritual and Psychological Interpretations:
Although these interpretations have been given to me via the spirit through experience and study, they are NOT absolute, but they will serve as a foundation for your spiritual discovery, understanding, enlightenment, and/or journey to new possibilities in the realm of the spirit.

Altar- This represents letting go of something or someone hindering your walk with God

Ancestors- This indicates that a healing process has taken place in your emotions as it relates to family members who have hurt you

Angel- God is attempting to get a special message to you

Apple- A sign of love, fertility, and the loss of earthly desires

Ant- A sign of diligence and organization

Automobile- A sign that the ego is out of control; something is amiss– lack of control, too much control, traveling too fast or too slow, taking the wrong direction in life

Baby- A rebirth of the self; the emergence of something new

Bag- Something that holds emotions, secrets, repressions, hopes, dreams, or desires; a bag denotes secrecy, regardless of its contents

Ball- A sign of wholeness or completeness

Bear- Resurrection, rebirth, or initiation

Bedroom- Sexual relations, sexual intimacy needed

Birds- God is about to take your mind, will, and emotions to another level

Blindness- Ignorance in a certain area

Blood- Something you're doing could cost you your life

Book- God is trying to reveal to you his wisdom and direction from the bible

Break-in- Someone is trying to come into

your life, but you don't need them in

Breast- A desire to be loved and nurtured

Bride- There is something wrong in your marriage that God is attempting to show you

Bridge- Making a transition from one place to another

Building- God is about to take you from one level to another

Bus- Travel from one place to another

Butterfly- You need to change something in your life

Cafeteria- A public place where adequate but uninspired food (spiritual) is served

Cancer- Dreams of having cancer probably don't concern the real illness, but rather symbolizing anxieties over a consuming problem

Candles- God is trying to reveal something to your mind that he has already revealed in your spirit

Cat- A need for love and intimacy

Chains- You're in bondage to something or someone and you need to be free

Chair- A need of support and rest; it also means power or authority that God is about to grant you

Children- Innocence, naïve, and immature

Church- God is attempting to show you where you need to join

Circle- A need for completion

Class- A need for more learning in a particular area

Climbing- A need to make the effort to overcome obstacles

Clock- God is attempting to show you that you're running out of time

Closet- You're trying to hide something that you and God need to talk about

Clothing- Your attempt to cover your flaws with clothes can be seen by the almighty

Clouds- Confusion and a state of complete unhappiness

Coffin- Something old and negative is about to be buried in your life

Court- Order needs to be restored in your life

Cow- God is attempting to deal with your maternal instincts; your motherhood

Cross- A symbol of death; someone you know is going to die

Crown- A sign of authority; sovereignty; mastery over one's self

Cup- A symbol of plenty and a sign of prosperity

Dancing- God is attempting to connect you to someone emotionally

Darkness- A sign of death and destruction

*The Death-*The appearance in a dream of a person who is dead is a sign of your grieving over someone who has either died or a relationship has ended

Death- Usually, dreams involving death are not literal warnings of impending physical death, but they represent the decay and destruction of a stage in life; an attachment that needs to die

Demon- A sign of sin and iniquity

Dog- A sign of a spiritual Shepard, one who guides the flock; loyalty and devotion

Doctor- A sign of healing; the gift of healing is about to manifest

Door- Opportunities and choices

Dove- A sign of the Holy Spirit

Drowning- Drowning symbolizes a sense of the loss of one's identity or ego, or of being overwhelmed by emotions

Eagle- Spiritual victory and material triumph

Ear- Receptivity and willingness to listen

Egg- A beginning; something new is about to come into your life

Eye- God wants you to see something you've been missing

Famous people- To associate with their accomplishments, failures, personalities, skills, talents, qualities, and faults

Fence- Barriers and confinement

Fight- Unresolved inner tensions

Fire- Purification, transformation, and illumination

Fish- God is about to save someone you thought would never be saved; birth

Flood- A flood is a sign of the end of an old phase in life

Flowers- A sign that something you've hated is about to become enjoyable

Flying- A sign that one is not struck or limited in life

Gate- You're about to go through something

Giant- Problems that are overpowering and out of control

Grave- You need to bury your old life and your past

Hair- Strength, vitality, and anointing

Hands- A sign that God is going to use you in a Ministry calling

Hell- You're doing something that is going to damn your soul

Journey- A sign of a spiritual quest

Key- A solution to a problem

Kiss- A sign that you're are about to be adored by someone special

Ladder- You are about to be exposed to the spirit world

Lamp- A sign of divine wisdom and guidance

Lion- A sign of strength and courage

Marriage- A coming together of opposites or a reconciliation of differences

Maze- To being in a state of confusion

Mirror- You need to take a closer look at yourself

Missing Transportation- A missed opportunity

Money- God is trying to show you your worth and value

Monsters- You've got some fears that need to be gotten rid of

Night- The unknown

Nudity- Vulnerability; openness; sincerity; embarrassment

Ocean- The unconscious

Old people- A sign of mature wisdom

Owl- A symbol of either wisdom or death

Packing- A sign that you need to leave

something or someone

Lamb- Dependent and vulnerable

Lion- A temper out of control

Monkey- Foolishness

Mouse- Sneaky

Pig- An appetite out of control

Rabbit- You need to get control of your sexual drive

Sheep- To be easily led into the wrong situations

Wolf- Someone is trying to deceive you

Bird- Get out of your nest; dependency

Black bird- Death

Chicken- An idea that needs to be born

Crow or Raven- Death

Dove- Peace

Eagle, Buzzard, Hawk- Patience

Owl- Death

Peacock- Too much pride

Boat ride- You're getting prepared to go through rough times

Blood- Relatives need prayer from danger

Burial or Funeral- Letting go of your past

Cancer- Fear of an illness

Devil- Something in your life has come under demonic control

Father- This image most always represents

God

Banana- Something needs to be stripped from your personality

Bath- Cleansing or a change of heart or a need to forgive

Bicycle- You're not going as fast as you should be going

Prison- Being confined, pinned down, limited in options ad activity

Quarrel- A mirror of an inner conflict

Quicksand- Something or someone is pulling you down with them

Rain- In dreams, any kind of contact with water can be seen as contact with the unconscious. When the unconscious comes to us in the form of rain, it is demanding our attention, perhaps seeking to engage us in something we have failed to recognize or have avoided.

Rainbow- A sign and symbol of a promise that God has made you

Rose- A symbol of eternity life

Salt- A sign of purity and the fact that God is going to preserve you through something

Snake- A sign of healing, wisdom, and deception

Snow- A sign of feelings, talents, or abilities

that have been frozen

Stairs- A sign that God wants you higher

Tears- A sign that your trouble or burden is about to leave

Violence- The beginning stage of a unique transformation

Water- A sign that God is about to drown something in your life; water is also a sign of the Word, perhaps you need to get in it more; God is about to wash something unclean out of your life with the Word

Wheel- A set pattern in your life is about to change; it also represents going around and around and getting nowhere

*Ape-*Wisdom

Bear- Possessiveness

Cat- Our spirit warning us of an unseen danger

Cow- You give yourself too easily to others

Dinosaur- Fear, reproduction, and survival

Dog- Devotion

Frog- You're getting ready for a shift or change

Goat- Repressed emotions

Horse- Fear of entering into love

Notes

_____

_____

_____

_____

_____

_____

_____

_____

_____

_____

_____

_____

_____

_____

_____

_____

_____

_____

_____

_____

_____

_____

_____

_____

The Conclusion

Anytime we are dealing with anything that's supernatural, we must become a student and be willing learn more every day! I pray this book helped you glean some insight concerning the supernatural portal of dreams. It is my prayer that you would take this information and revelation and pass it on because there are so many in the world that are in need of this teaching on this subject. I bless you my brother and my sister! May the Lord bless thee, may the Lord keep thee, may the Lord lift up his countenance on thee and give thee peace! May you discover more things in God as you pursue the things of the spirit! Shalom and Amen!

ABOUT THE AUTHOR

APOSTLE **C. A. TURNER** is the prophetic voice for this last hour. He is the Senior Pastor and Founder of Kingdom Nation Ministries and About Gods Business World Outreach ministries in Jonesboro, AR and Memphis, TN. He has been preaching and teaching for over 25 years, reaching the lost at all cost and impacting the earth with the things concerning the kingdom of God with miracles, signs, and wonders operating within his ministry. He attended Grambling State University with a focus in Business

Administration. He also Attended the School of Exodus studying Theology and Biblical Studies. He is the founder of Y.E.S.S. Young Entrepreneur Success School for the urban youth with a focus in financial Literacy. Carlos Turner is the owner and CEO of several successful businesses, Kingdom Clean Detailing, Tojoe's Wings and Waffles, Turner and Thomas Real Estate, Carlo Avery Fashions, and Olive Tree Finance and Investment Firm. In his spare time, he loves reading, studying, and researching the things of the spirit to stay sharp and alert for the things to come! His favorite verse is found in the book of Luke 1:37 that says, "For with God nothing shall be impossible!" His assignment is to shake and reawaken the body of Christ in the area of the supernatural. He understands that this will be a life journey, so he is totally committed to the things of God and strictly being about God's Business.

J. Kenkade
PUBLISHING®

Our Motto
"Transforming Life Stories"

Publish Your Book With Us

Our All-Inclusive Self-Publishing Packages

100% Royalties
Professional Proofreading & Editing
Interior Design & Cover Design
Self-Publishing Tutorial & More

For Manuscript Submission or other inquiries:
www.jkenkadepublishing.com
(501) 482-JKEN

Also Available from
J. Kenkade Publishing

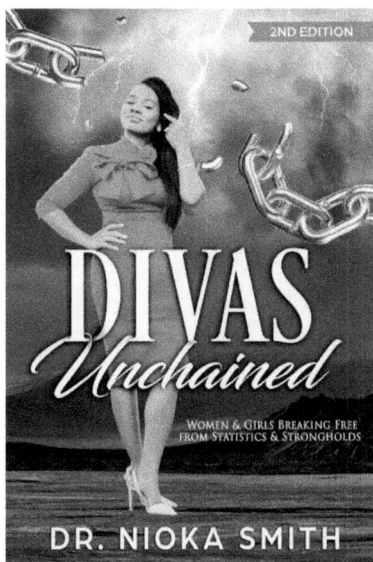

ISBN: 978-1-944486-25-9
Visit www.drniokasmith.com
Author: Dr. Nioka Smith

Sexually abused by her father at the age of 14, pregnant at the age of 17, and a nervous breakdown at the age of 28, Dr. Nioka Smith's painful past almost killed her, until the voice of the Lord guided her into destroying strongholds and reversing Satan's plan for her life. DIVAS Unchained is the powerful chain-breaking reality of the many unfortunate strongholds our women and girls face. Dr. Nioka uses her divine gift to help women and girls break free from destructive life cycles and prosper in all areas of life. Satan has lied to you. It's time to expose his lies. It's time to break free!

Also Available from
J. Kenkade Publishing

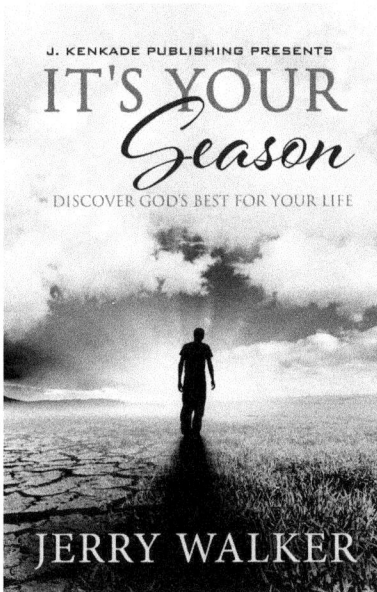

ISBN: 978-1-944486-72-3
Visit www.amazon.com
Author: Jerry Walker

Do you find yourself asking the question, "Is there more to life than the seemingly never-ending struggle of survival?" This book answers that question with a resounding, "YES!" Jesus died to give us MORE. Jerry Walker has written this manual for Christian living that gives in-depth teaching on scripture and how to apply it to your life. Full of tools for living a life of freedom in Christ, this book will be a blessing to all who read it. Your time is now, it truly is your season!

Also Available from J. Kenkade Publishing

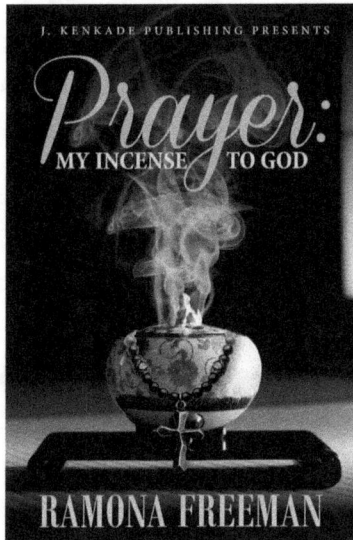

ISBN: 978-1-944486-65-5
Visit www.amazon.com
Author: Ramona Freeman

"Prayer: My Incense to God" is a composition of prayers created by the author over the years for various topics. The purpose of this prayer manual is to set a foundation of prayer and intercession according to the Word of God, to establish prayer in every home, city, state, and nation, and to pray the will of God in order to see His kingdom come on Earth as it is in Heaven (Matthew 6:10).

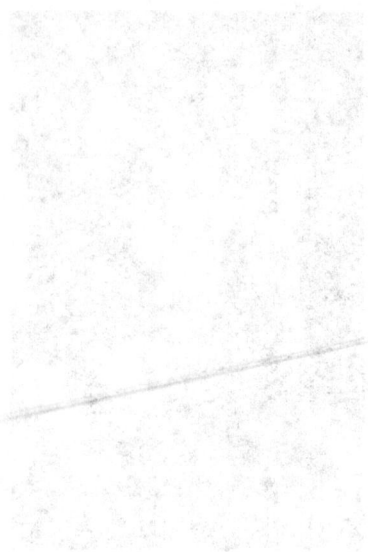

Also Available from
J. Kenkade Publishing

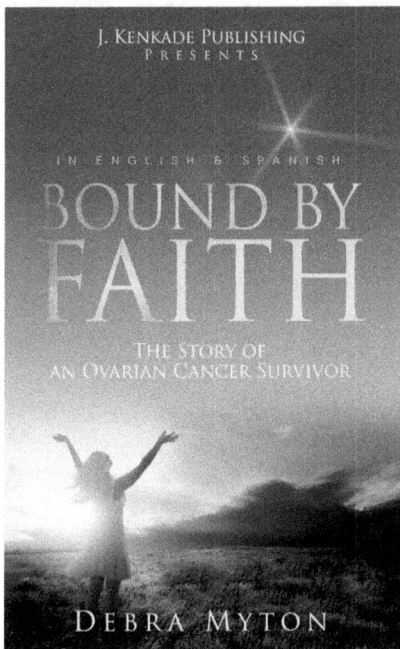

ISBN: 978-1-944486-20-4
Visit www.amazon.com
Author: Debra Myton

As a school counselor and mother, the author became extremely concerned about her ovarian cancer diagnosis, nutrition, and weight loss. Research shows that people do not get second opinions about their health, although health professionals do not see second opinions as a breach of trust from people. This book is a personal guide on how to handle any illness that a man or woman may face in life. This personal cancer story will make you laugh, cry, but overall, will empower you by faith. Join Debra in her journey of survival in "Bound by Faith".

www.ingramcontent.com/pod-product-compliance
Lightning Source LLC
LaVergne TN
LVHW051139080426
835508LV00021B/2704